Table of Contents

Consultant Note

"On It, Phonics!" is designed to reinforce vowel sounds, beginning blends, and sight words and to provide reading practice for young readers. Books like these are one important part of a comprehensive literacy program for students at emergent and beginning levels. "On It, Phonics!" should be used with other high-quality children's books. Instructors and parents are advised to go over the words in the picture glossary before students begin reading, and review the sight words after students finish reading. You can also ask students to go back and identify words with the target letter-sound.

Andrew P. Johnson, PhD,
Distinguished Faculty Scholar and
Professor of Literacy Instruction,
Minnesota State University, Mankato

BL Blend Picture Glossary

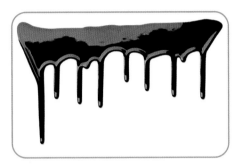

black

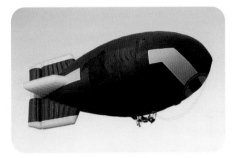

blimp

block

blue

Black and Blue

Black and blue are colors.

Is this block blue?

Yes, this block is blue.

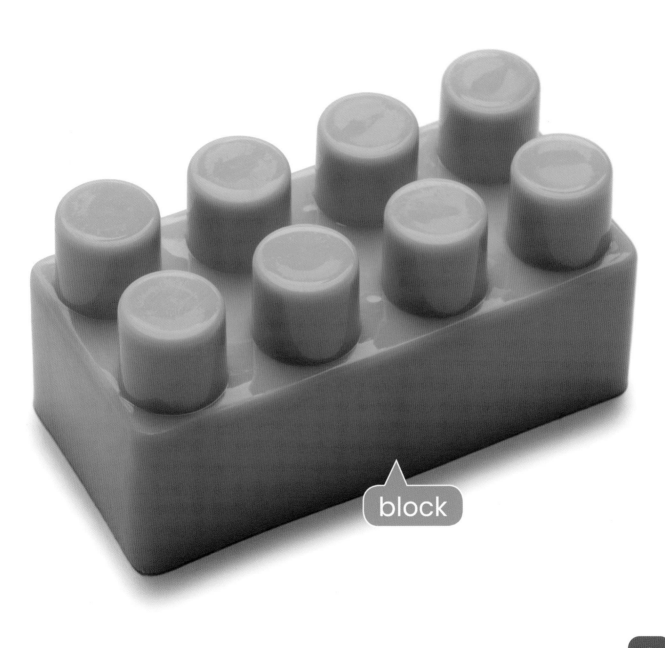

block

Is this block black?

Yes, this block is black.

block

Is this blimp black?

Yes, this blimp is black.

Is this blimp blue?

Yes, this blimp is blue.

Is this bird blue?

Yes, this bird is blue.

bird

Is this bird black?

Yes, this bird is black.

Is this ball blue?

Yes, this ball is blue.

Is this ball black?

Yes, this ball is black.

ball

Sight Words

and
are
black
blue
is
this
yes